CHINESE MYTHOLOGY

Chang'e
Goddess of the Moon

BY JEAN KUO LEE

CONTENT CONSULTANT
GANG LIU, PHD
ASSOCIATE TEACHING PROFESSOR
CARNEGIE MELLON UNIVERSITY

Kids Core
An Imprint of Abdo Publishing
abdobooks.com

abdobooks.com

Printed in the United States of America, North Mankato, Minnesota.
102022
012023

THIS BOOK CONTAINS RECYCLED MATERIALS

Cover Photo: Photo Researchers/Science History Images/Alamy
Interior Photos: Pictures From History/CPA Media Pte Ltd/Alamy, 4–5, 29 (top); Historica Graphica Collection/Heritage Image Partnership Ltd /Alamy, 6, 28 (top); The Picture Art Collection/Alamy, 8; Shutterstock Images, 10, 16, 21 (top left); Yixian/Alamy, 12–13; John Stevenson/Asian Art & Archaeology Inc./Corbis Historical/Getty Images, 14, 28 (bottom); STR/AFP/Getty Images, 18–19; S. Dali/Shutterstock Images, 21 (map); Benjamin B./Shutterstock Images, 21 (top middle); Mau Horng/Shutterstock Images, 21 (top right); Romix Image/Shutterstock Images, 21 (bottom left); Boontoom Sae-Kor/Shutterstock Images, 21 (bottom right); Phoebe Yu/iStockphoto, 22, 29 (bottom); Heritage Art/Heritage Images/Hulton Archive/Getty Images, 24; iStockphoto, 26

Editor: Ann Schwab
Series Designer: Ryan Gale

Library of Congress Control Number: 2022940675

Publisher's Cataloging-in-Publication Data

Names: Lee, Jean Kuo, author.
Title: Chang'e: Goddess of the Moon / by Jean Kuo Lee
Description: Minneapolis, Minnesota: Abdo Publishing, 2023 | Series: Chinese Mythology | Includes online resources and index.
Identifiers: ISBN 9781532199929 (lib. bdg.) | ISBN 9781098275129 (ebook)
Subjects: LCSH: Deities--Juvenile literature. | Gods, Chinese--Juvenile literature. | Mythology, Chinese--Juvenile literature.
Classification: DDC 299.51--dc23

CONTENTS

Stories about Chang'e appear in many myths, poems, and novels.

CHAPTER 1

The Spirit of the Moon

Once there was a hero in ancient China. His name was Hou Yi. He saved people with his great deeds. For a reward, he asked the goddess Xiwangmu for an **elixir** of **immortality**. If he drank the potion, he would live forever.

After Chang'e flew to the moon, she and Hou Yi were separated forever.

He was granted the elixir and gave it to his wife, Chang'e. She would keep it safe for him. But someone broke into their home and tried to steal it. Chang'e swallowed the potion and escaped to the sky. She now lives on the moon.

This story of Chang'e is the most famous version of the Chinese myth today. It says Chang'e saved the potion from the thief. She became the spirit of the moon.

Hou Yi: Chinese Hero

Hou Yi was the best **archer** in the world. One year, ten suns rose in the sky. The extreme heat was burning the land. Crops died, so there was no food. To save people from suffering, Hou Yi shot down nine of the suns. Afterward, the goddess Xiwangmu gave him a gift that would let him live forever. This was the elixir of immortality.

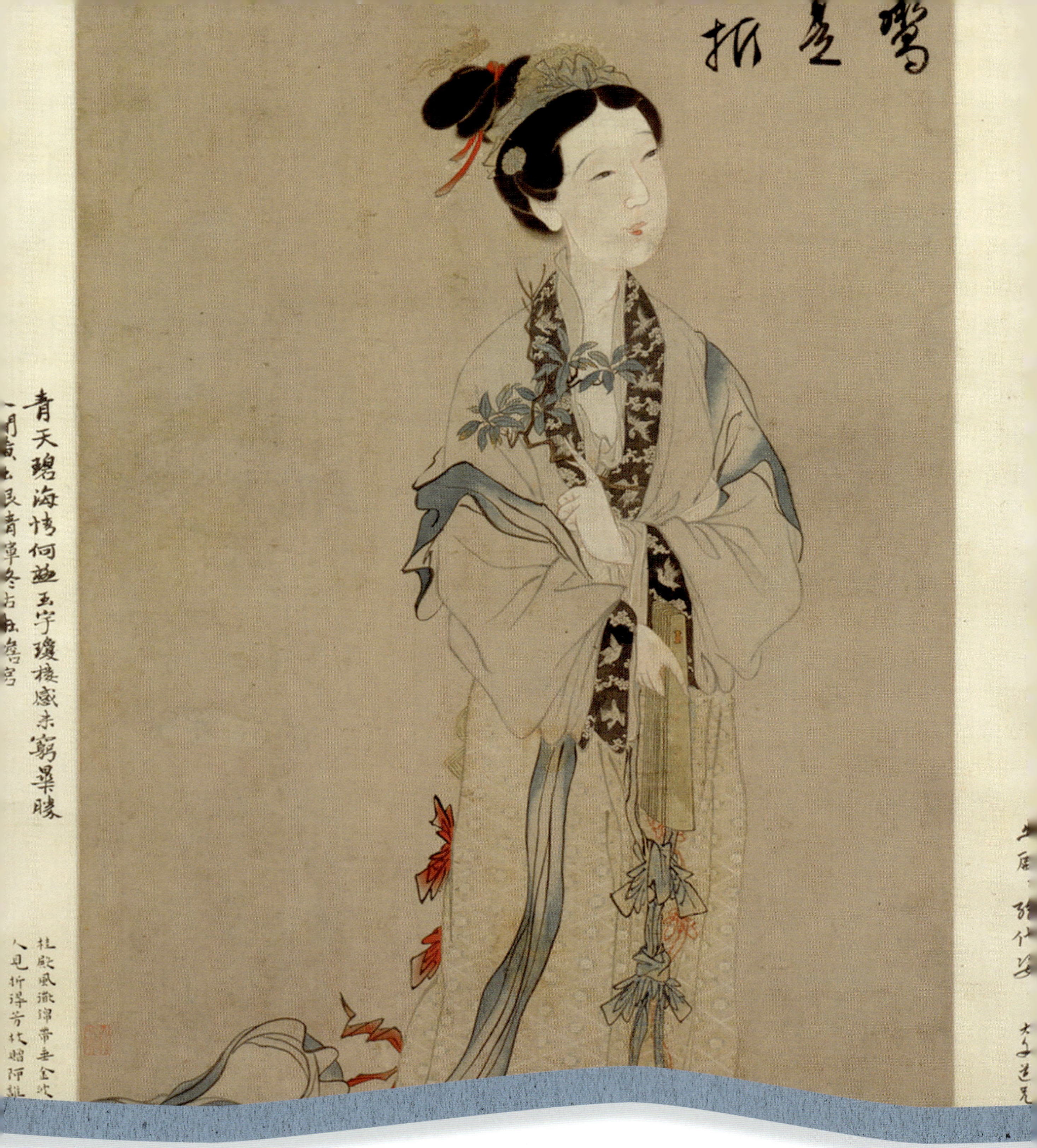

Myths about Chang'e have been told for a very long time. This painting of her was created hundreds of years ago.

Chang'e's husband honored her with a tradition. Once a year, he offered her favorite cakes and fruits to the moon. He did this on the day that the moon is fullest and brightest, hoping to see his wife's shadow. It was a way to remember her kindness and her good deed.

But there are other versions of the Chang'e myth. Stories about her first appeared 2,500 years ago. In all versions, she took her husband's elixir and flew to the moon. But the stories do not agree on why this happened.

In the myths, Chang'e became known as the goddess of the moon.

What Is Chinese Mythology?

Chinese myths are stories from ancient times. They often mix history with legends. Many stories are about gods and goddesses.

The people of China recorded myths in ancient writings. The earliest writings are from about 3,000 years ago. Chinese people told these stories to each other. They continue to tell them today. Some stories are examples of good behavior to follow. Some are told as bad examples to avoid. The stories have changed over time to fit the reason they are being told.

Further Evidence

Look at the website below. Does it give any new evidence to support Chapter One?

Mythology

abdocorelibrary.com/chang'e

Chang'e's story has captivated people for centuries.

CHAPTER 2

The Beautiful Moon Goddess

In recent stories, Chang'e is a symbol of beauty and grace. She is quiet and gentle. In paintings and novels, she is charming. But in the earliest versions, the story of Chang'e is different.

Chang'e is joined on the moon by the woodcutter Wu Gang.

The first stories say Chang'e stole the elixir from her husband so she could be immortal. After she drank the elixir, she flew to the moon.

In some versions of the tale, Chang'e is punished for her crime. She is compelled to drink the elixir for all time. Using a **mortar and pestle**, she smashes the ingredients to make the potion. She must continue to make the elixir forever.

Moon Companions

Chang'e's neighbor on the moon is Wu Gang. He was banished there for wrongdoing. He must chop down a tree on the moon. But the bark keeps healing itself. He is forever chopping but never able to cut the tree down.

In later stories, a rabbit joins Chang'e on the moon. Called the Jade Rabbit, it befriends Chang'e, pounding the elixir for her.

The Jade Rabbit is featured in many versions of Chang'e's story.

Now, the myth of Chang'e shows her as a beautiful goddess on the moon. She does no work and receives no punishment.

Who Is the Jade Rabbit?

In Chinese tales, the shadow on the moon is of a rabbit. One story says the Jade Emperor, a god, was very pleased at how well the rabbit created the elixir. So he made its fur as beautiful as jade. The animal became known as the Jade Rabbit.

PRIMARY SOURCE

The Chinese poet Li Shangyin (813–858 CE) wrote about Chang'e in his poem, "To the Moon Goddess":

> *Are you sorry for having stolen the potion*
> *that has set you*
> *Over purple seas and blue skies, to brood*
> *through the long nights?*

Source: Li Shangyin. "To the Moon Goddess." *300 Tang Poems*, edited by Heng-t'ang-t'ui-Shih, Alfred A. Knopf, 1920, xtf.lib.virginia.edu, n.d. Accessed 8 Apr. 2022.

Point of View

What is the author's point of view on this topic? What is your point of view? Write a short essay about how they are similar and different.

Colorful lanterns fill the streets of Shanghai, China, as people celebrate the Mid-Autumn Festival.

CHAPTER 3

Honoring Chang'e

On the night of the year when the full moon is brightest and fullest, Chinese families celebrate a tradition. They picnic in the garden under the **harvest moon**. The special event is called the Mid-Autumn Festival.

Families eat moon cakes. These are pastry treats that have a round shape like a full moon. There are many different types of moon cakes. Some have a sweet filling. Others are filled with pork or sausage. Families often share a single moon cake. They also eat round fruits such as apples and pomegranates. The round shape, like the full moon, symbolizes togetherness. A full moon also represents wealth and unity for the family. Parents tell the story of Chang'e to their children to honor her. People often give moon cakes as gifts to friends and neighbors too.

Moon Cakes

Different regions of China feature special kinds of moon cakes. Here are some of the moon cakes enjoyed during the Mid-Autumn Festival.

The ancient stories say that Hou Yi placed moon cakes out for Chang'e during the harvest moon. This is when the moon appears to be closest to Earth.

Some say the Mid-Autumn Festival first began with Hou Yi. He held a ceremony for Chang'e on the day of the full moon in autumn. This was on the fifteenth day of the eighth month in the lunar calendar. Others began to follow his example every year, and it became a tradition.

At this time, East Asian farmers also celebrate the **harvest** of rice and wheat. They give thanks for the fruits of their labor. They rest and look at the beauty of the moon.

What Is the Lunar Calendar?

In a solar calendar, the months of the year are based on the time it takes Earth to make one trip around the Sun. In a lunar calendar, used in ancient China, the months follow the cycles of the moon's phases. Today, most Chinese people use a solar calendar. However, the dates of Chinese festivals still follow the lunar calendar.

Chang'e and her story have been celebrated in many paintings and other forms of art.

The Mid-Autumn Festival is also celebrated in other Asian countries, such as South Korea, Vietnam, and Malaysia. In parts of the world that don't use the lunar calendar, the festival falls in September or early October.

Chang'e in Art

For thousands of years, Chinese people have decorated moon cakes with pictures of Chang'e. Today, she appears on moon cake boxes alongside a full moon. Artists sometimes show her under a cassia tree or holding the Jade Rabbit. She also appears in paintings, cartoons, paper cuttings, and other art forms. She is even featured in an animated movie.

Chang'e is one of the most popular and beloved Chinese goddesses.

During the Mid-Autumn Festival, many families honor Chang'e. They hang a painting of her on the wall. Or they might decorate with a clay statue of the Jade Rabbit.

The ancient Chinese told many versions of the Chang'e myth. Poets and novelists write about her. Today, Chinese people continue to tell these stories every year during the Mid-Autumn Festival. They honor Chang'e as a symbol of female beauty and grace.

Explore Online

Visit the website below. Does it give new information about the Mid-Autumn Festival that wasn't in Chapter Three?

How the World Celebrates Mid-Autumn Festival

abdocorelibrary.com/chang'e

LEGENDARY FACTS

Chang'e drank her husband's elixir and escaped to the moon.

Chang'e's neighbor on the moon is Wu Gang.

Chang'e is considered the spirit of the moon, symbolizing beauty and grace.

Chang'e is honored every year during the Mid-Autumn Festival.

Glossary

archer
a person skilled at using a bow and arrow

elixir
a liquid mixture used as a medicine; often, it refers to a substance that prolongs life forever

harvest
the act of gathering crops

harvest moon
a full moon that happens in September or October

immortality
living forever

mortar and pestle
a bowl and pounding tool used to grind something into powder

Online Resources

To learn more about Chang'e and Chinese mythology, visit our free resource websites below.

Core Library CONNECTION
FREE! COMMON CORE MULTIMEDIA RESOURCES

Visit **abdocorelibrary.com** or scan this QR code for free Common Core resources for teachers and students, including vetted activities, multimedia, and booklinks, for deeper subject comprehension.

Booklinks NONFICTION NETWORK
FREE! ONLINE NONFICTION RESOURCES

Visit **abdobooklinks.com** or scan this QR code for free additional online weblinks for further learning. These links are routinely monitored and updated to provide the most current information available.

Learn More

Hamby, Zachary. *Introduction to Mythology for Kids: Legendary Stories from around the World.* Rockridge, 2020.

Wilhelm, Richard, and Frederick H. Martens. *Chinese Fairy Tales and Legends.* Bloomsbury China, 2019.

Index

About the Author

Jean Kuo Lee is a Chinese American writer. She writes fiction and nonfiction books for curious kids.